THE MOSAIC

THE MOSAIC
A Collection of Poems

SWATI CHOPRA

Published by
Rupa Publications India Pvt. Ltd 2024
7/16, Ansari Road, Daryaganj
New Delhi 110002

Sales centres:
Bengaluru Chennai Hyderabad
Jaipur Kathmandu Kolkata
Mumbai Prayagraj

Copyright © Swati Chopra 2024

All rights reserved.
No part of this publication may be reproduced, transmitted,
or stored in a retrieval system, in any form or by any means,
electronic, mechanical, photocopying, recording or otherwise,
without the prior permission of the publisher.

P-ISBN: 978-93-5702-946-9
E-ISBN: 978-93-90260-80-5

First impression 2024

10 9 8 7 6 5 4 3 2 1

The moral right of the author has been asserted.

Printed in India

This book is sold subject to the condition that it shall not, by way of
trade or otherwise, be lent, resold, hired out, or otherwise circulated,
without the publisher's prior consent, in any form of binding or
cover other than that in which it is published.

To my Mother, my Father and my Guru

Contents

Preface	*xi*
1. A Curious Child	1
2. Dark Unknown Lives	2
3. Barrierless!	4
4. Gender: A Non-synergized Concept	5
5. One Constant and One Variable	6
6. In Anticipation	7
7. Path…Where Art Thou!	8
8. Alas, the Daughter Today!	10
9. Human Nature	12
10. Caged Existence	13
11. India's Crossroads	14
12. The Need for a Global Corrective Action	15
13. A Rainbow Called Life	17
14. A Kaleidoscope Called Life	18
15. Extremes	19
16. Love: A Mysticism?	20
17. The Divine Space	21

18. A Mirror Called Life	22
19. Beauty	24
20. To Be or Not to Be	25
21. Circus of Life	26
22. And the Clock Had Ticked	27
23. Reflections on Bureaucracy	28
24. Indifferent Mysticism	30
25. Journey of the Soul	31
26. The World Ahead	32
27. The Nilgiris: A Deeper Experience	33
28. Cacophony	34
29. The Wildlife	36
30. The World Looks So Wide	37
31. Buddies	38
32. Beckoning the Indian Women	40
33. The Five Elements of Life	42
34. Fallacies Fade	44
35. Oh Warrior!	45
36. Safe, at Last	46
37. Your Gratuity	47
38. Your Grandeur!	48
39. Transformation	49

40. Are We Guilty?	50
41. Nature's Release	51
42. The Fathomable Spirit	52
43. Change, No Alternative	53
44. It Is for Us Only	54
45. Primitive: An Era Evergreen	55
46. A New Way of Life	56
47. Eyes that Couldn't See	57
48. The Predestined Meeting	58
49. Longingness Revisited	59
50. Is the Path Ahead Backwards?	60
51. Another Dimension	62
52. Life: A Meandering River	63
53. The Sun at Dawn	64
54. Significance of Rain	66
55. Mankind: Yet to Arrive	67
56. Let Me be Your Light	68
57. Art Forms	69
58. Institutions	70
59. Life: Certainty versus Uncertainty	71
60. Social or Unsocial Media?	72
61. Keep Your Spirit High	74

62. Quarantine Reflections I	76
63. Quarantine Reflections II	81
64. Love in the Times of Covid-19	82
65. Discriminate Covid-19, Not Its Warriors	84
66. A Deeper Meaning	85
67. Blissful Praise	87
68. A Yearning Soul	89
69. The River: The Ocean	91
70. Playfulness	93
71. Why?	94
72. March of the Feminine	96
73. Twin Saga	97
74. Ignorance is Bliss	98
75. Life from Pram to Wheelchair	99
Acknowledgements	100

Preface

'The Mosaic' is a name that truly encompasses the very essence of this selective poetry. As I present to you my first book of poems, I must admit that these poems were initially never written with an intention to publish them. However, gradually it touched more readers in my circle and the need to publish them came organically. These 75 poems vary in their dimensions from abstract and current affairs, to humanity, spirituality, feminism, motivation and so forth. Many of these are an introspection of life from my prism of mind as various muses struck the chords of my heart from time to time. These verses are from the very depths of my soul. I thank all the people who have inspired me to write them and the Almighty who woke me up in the middle of nights to put them on paper. I sincerely hope true lovers of poetry will enjoy reading them. Thank you!

1

A Curious Child

Another attempt merely a step closer to decipher You,
In the vastness of this eternity I seek You.
Like a child playing with small pebbles by the ocean,
'What is it?' an engraved voice calls out its slogan.

At times, we appear insignificant in Your creation,
At times, we gain strength to uncover and reason.
To predict the randomness of the Universe so complex,
I hope we are not merely small pearls lost in Your closet.

Even the predictors have their own doubts in life,
How helpless and lost they feel in this strife.
My mind always concludes the same every time.
Hail you Almighty, Your creation—all Thine!

2

Dark Unknown Lives

Words fall short or perhaps shy away,
To describe these lives—I will attempt, if I may?
Far away from the maddening crowd of the city
These are unspoken, untold lives, what a pity!

In a deep, dark tunnel they live
Their sole purpose of existence is to 'give'.
To give food to their crying children and just be there,
To offer flesh to those wolves and just be there.

They have been allocated perhaps four or five steps,
In those steps they live their valuable life.
We say that Earth has enough for everybody's need,
Perhaps, they don't know there is a territory beyond.

What is this plight? Why the bias?
You have devised this plan for them,
You have pushed them into this den.
My heart bleeds to see this—where are You then?

They are married off for a few acres of land,
Then why only an area of vegetables are they lent?
This is not fair at all—this is unethical and immoral
Why are you so quiet—my soul alone quarrels!

This inertia of ages maintains its status quo,
With your support, they just blindly tread and go.
The soul of this motherland is in decay,
Disheartening is the picture of this world not so gay.

Doesn't your soul hurt letting things just be?
Doesn't your eye shed a tear, oh thee?
Doesn't your hand rise when someone uses their evil hand?
Doesn't your ear hurt when you hear their cries?
Doesn't your feet stand against the feet that kick?
Oh Lord! A chill runs down my spine to see all this!

3

Barrierless!

I want to fly in the sky, swim against the ocean
And break all the barriers of convention.
My soul knows no bounds if unleashed once,
That moment has to come one day—nay a trance.

When the world has no restrictions for you,
That day will come—it is definitely true.
Why do we live a life of fear and what ifs?
Why are we so tied down to our self-made cliffs?

I want my energies to travel across the Universe
Even while I write this, into an unending growing
    space I disperse.
Do something worthwhile for souls similar to mine
With surrender, oh Lord—I pray unto thine!

4

Gender: A Non-synergized Concept

In verses, my unseen and unmanifest pours out.
All that softness and vulnerability loses its stout.
How concealed are we from the world around us?
All seem lost in the thoughts of chase and lust.

My ideals come into conflict in this patriarchal world,
I was brought up with a clean slate—with no sadness ever hurled.
Why does the lady always have to be the giver?
Will this notion of sickness mend ever?

I wish I come across men of stature and consciousness
Faraway, towards truth, untouched by all callousness.
You created all with the same elements and energy
Then why on gender has the world lost its synergy?

One Constant and One Variable

In different phases of life, I seek you,
Every time a changed me, a constant you.
Nothing permanent, except this
Nothing but 'you' is indeed true!

What changes are the answers I get
To questions I posed when we met.
I move ahead on my journey in this eternity,
Every part of it I take as a step towards self-purity.

It's time for farewell and congratulations
As I shun my old thinking, old habits, old *sanskara*s
Into the new I walk—perhaps, crawling at the
    moment
Seeking this path with people of varied auras.

I must move past to reflect on 'why' this unfurled,
Thill then, I pray for strength in my trembling world.

In Anticipation

Time is passing, just flying away
There is an inherent silence drifting me away.
From the noise of this existing illusion,
Take me to a place with a greater conclusion.

Help me hear what the birds have to say,
Let me observe and contemplate a new day.
Bless me to see the rainbow's colours in a ray,
Let the shadows to the sun, now fall as a prey.

Let the clouds now have a downpour of heaviness,
Let the moon inspire beauty and romance,
Let the fears and ambiguity vanish forever
For the prestige of your time and grace.

Help me now, to come out of this maze!

Path... Where Art Thou!

'Ah, what a creation!' God would have exclaimed,
After marvelling at the rare species that He had made.
To maintain harmony of His varied creations he is apt,
To any situation in the entire ecosystem he can adapt.

How sad is the situation in the present day,
'Man' is on a verge of collapse and gradual decay.
His own health is endangered, while he works on Red Lists,
A pack of fallen cards is his life in a gist.

Power hungry, unsatisfied relationships, diseases and all,
He is sadly on the brink of his fall.
Intellect, wisdom, vision—all his remarkable attributes,
He is now paying for his acts of moral turpitude!

Where lies the path ahead of human race, oh Lord!
Please tie him back to Your umbilical cord.
Restore the equilibrium—even through his mistakes,
Pardon mankind I plead, something else You may forsake!

8

Alas, the Daughter Today!

She comes in like a fragrance, a sweet melody,
Filling lives with blessings selflessly.
The world exclaims, 'Ah, what a lovely baby!'
She will surely grow up to be a warrior lady.

Time flies, her strengths tested by the world around her,
Studies, sports, debates and aesthetics surround her.
Naturally gifted talents make the blessed soul known to all,
There, she emerges victorious, shinning tall.

She moves ahead on the path of her life,
Battling every situation for her family's might.
She attracts all the fortunes—wealth, power, prestige and happiness,
Until 'the day' she becomes someone's wife.

All accolades take a back seat
After all, it's a 'daughter's wedding, when the family should be cooked like a meat.

We also have to give lots to her in-laws,
After all, she is going under their claws.

She says, 'No need to do all this, please,
All this is giving my victories a tease.'
No, No, No, for God's sake everybody,'
'You relax, we will have to do this,' says her Daddy.

She won all battles of her life fearlessly,
She was taught to be this way—what a tragedy.
Today, all her struggles in one stroke become a farce.
What is this society we have created, let's pause!

Where are we heading with this paradox,
Which is making us humans worse than dogs.
Why this pretence of equality and empowerment,
When it is just another device of mere entrenchment.

The equally tall figure now stands short,
Hurt with deceit of values, culture and morality—
    what a flaw!
Oh Lord, let her remain triumphant for she shall
    always be.
As she prays for a world true and free!

Human Nature

'Human Nature'—a magnificent creation of this Universe
Nothing could be categorically said though eras you may traverse!
The inherent duality of the material and spiritual,
Landing up always in an area of life—ever critical!

The desire to have the best of both worlds,
The thirst for knowledge and greed for pleasure,
The want of success without any failure,
The yearning for popularity, the need for solitude.

The desire for beauty, the sadness of it without brains,
The time to walk, amongst the bullet trains!
The fire for name, yet the freedom of namelessness.
The institutions of culture, the spirit of tamelessness.

Caged Existence

*I*ntentionally mystified, deliberately caricaturized
How craftily has this method been devised?
Generating an area of tacit consent,
What more can a chauvinistic man want to invent?

Where did the brightness of Her life go?
She has been forced to ape someone else's toe!
While suffering in silence for over centuries
    together,
Why didn't you put up your strengths together?

Why was it left on externalities to change the plight?
You should have broken out, lashed out and put up a
    fight.
Today, as we enter a new domain of existence,
Shed the past and wake up, is my insistence!

11

India's Crossroads

A band of young upright officers march on,
With innovation on their mind, immensely strong.
At this junction of India's unprecedented transition,
We need true solutions, not the West's imitation.

After an era of Independence, debated over so long,
With talks, we cannot let the situation prolong.
Patriotism and sincerity are two indispensable values,
For at the end of the road, we will all have our dues.

A country that reigned supreme for centuries
    together,
With imperialism's blow, lost its gilded colour.
It must rise, and it will, beyond doubt.
We must not ignore the silver lining around the
    cloud!

12

The Need for a Global Corrective Action

In this web of complications, devised by intellectuals,
Is there a point to being too factual?
How many world's problems have we mitigated?
How many nations have smiled after being exasperated?

Has this system of haves and have-nots been intentionally drawn?
In chess, some nations are in the ruling and the others pawn.
Many know the solutions to this predicament,
However, implementers are on the flip side of this temperament.

What is my role in this eternal phenomenon?
Will I manifest on this side or the other?

Will this enthusiasm gain momentum or merely
   wither?
In context of the unfurling events,
I reflect on this thought so dual!

⁂

13

A Rainbow Called Life

As light traverses through the shade,
Various images, reflections and spectacles are made,
The light compared to the soul invites its story,
Nay another imagination of mind—a rhetoric!

At the core lies a strong, pure energy,
The battery of power, the engine of the ship,
It is the life force—the moment till the tip,
It rests deep inside a reservoir, balancing with all
    energy.

It moves through the pre-embellished patterns of
    mind,
Carried through the various steps of the past times,
Its debits and credits make a mosaic around,
The presence of the two components can rarely be
    segregated.

A Kaleidoscope Called Life

I run, I try to move ahead, I try to break away from
   the past.
Yet you throw me back again to the last.
Please soften your stance on me, oh Lord!
I ain't a superwoman, just a little petal, oh Lord!

How will I survive, how far will I go?
What if this caravan suddenly takes a stop.
An exchange of the lasts and the firsts?
A shaking equilibrium goes to mope.

A replacement of tears with happiness,
A reaction bitter and sweet at the same time.
With this catalyst of relationships in these
   amalgamations,
This mosaic thrives—as I rotate the kaleidoscope
   called life!

15

Extremes

Still waters run deep, so do they run profound,
In peaceful times, no one can predict,
Is this the column of that sea floor that high?
In uncertainty and randomness we thrive.

Something so pleasant, so beautiful to behold,
Of stories, of paradises, of praises untold.
Alas, mystery and surprise—an iron lies beneath the gold,
These memories and experiences in life's cupboard you fold.

What is life? It is a dark, black box
At a moment, simultaneously hot and cold.
This dichotomy cuts through intersections of our lives,
Alas! People and relationships are both wax and knives.

16
Love: A Mysticism?

Does true love exist in reality or only in poems and stories?
Is there truly someone especially made for you?
Someone who makes you feel feminine,
Who brings out the best in you—a feeling divine!

With just an eye contact, you can see through your life,
Of the scars on the soul, of the heaviness in heart,
Of the soulful cries, of the hurtful emotions,
Of the true you, of the deep down loving you.

A touch of your hand—brief and intense,
Makes a million volts of divine energy spark,
A healing of every pain, moderation of excess rain,
A feeling of freshness and inspiration mysterious!

Someone whom you want to talk to, as he hears,
For he reflects and understands the unsaid words!

The Divine Space

*H*old me back sometimes, oh Lord!
Pull the strings of the soul softly,
Let me experience the divine freedom,
Of the unheard, untold story of thy kingdom.

In the limitations of worldly births,
Lies the infinite bliss of a stage mysterious,
In this vast electromagnetic space around,
There is one unknown flash of imagination.

You sense it sometimes, mostly it is indifferent,
This experience is something you won't ever lament,
To put it down in words is like trying
To break the bond which is always tying.

18

A Mirror Called Life

Untiringly and steadily, I walk ahead on the path,
All I have now is my faith,
Nothing but unhappiness with the present,
As my heart's desires run, looking at the night's
    crescent.

Sometimes all you have is an intuition,
Sometimes all you lose is your worst fear,
Sometimes all that life offers you is no choice,
Sometimes all you need to construct is a
    destruction.

Strange are the ways of life,
All that it follows is randomness and cacophony.
You have to catch it in a jiffy when it takes a turn,
A bitter pill, or a painful moment makes you learn.

You feel you control your life and path,
That very minute the destiny unfolds what has never
    been taught,
Before you are attuned or can balance yourself out,
It is already heading for another dramatic bout!

19

Beauty

*T*he first ray of the sun that mesmerizes,
The brightness of the night that lights up,
The tease of both the heart and soul,
As if every note is silently playing its role!

It is a reflection of the mysterious unknown,
A divine answer to the question of the manifest,
To appreciate its existence in a limitless eternity,
Is trying to define what cannot be constricted.

It is a blessing of the celestial and the Absolute,
Of romance and hope to the unfortunate and
    destitute,
The more you try holding the less you would,
To sum up in one pristine word—'Touchwood'!

To Be or Not to Be

The tides of life accede and recede,
Into the depths of significance and insignificance,
The soul takes its dip—a part of the plan
The question is—to be or not be?

In this interplay of consciousness with births and
    deaths
To apply these energies with a play of breath,
There is always something more to be known,
To decouple, maybe couple; to demystify only to seek
    to mystify.

Juxtaposed with these inklings of spiritualism that
    materialize
I move on my little journey through the universe,
Where do I stand, what do I stand for and why do I
    have to?
These curiosities play—I know not why!

Circus of Life

*I*n this circus of life, various elements interplay,
In the incompleteness of blending acts
Lies a bittersweet portrayal of emotions successively,
Partially true and partially false, ambidextrously.

How well do the wicked and the beautiful act
As per the script destined by the Master.
Some get so involved, yet others have nothing to
     fear,
We all play our fabricated parts—perhaps for a
     meagre.

The circus moves through eternity,
We act, laugh, cry, scorn, dance, appreciate it all,
Perform our bit and move on to new roles or no
     roles,
This is how the circus of life unfurls!

22

And the Clock Had Ticked

I met you, somewhere in a trance,
For a few split seconds in a dance,
As if I had known you since inception,
Or was it just my figurative deception?

I could not recollect even a frame before,
My hand resting on yours, moved.
It was as if I had to get back somewhere,
The meeting time was over—the clock had ticked.

The prerequisite to leave was the promise to
    converge,
The longing to connect yet does emerge.
I met as if the separation was a beginning,
That melody in my life is still lingering.

23

Reflections on Bureaucracy

You move ahead, thinking you are unique,
Having achieved various daunting feats,
Battling your fears and adversities,
Till you reach up to your bestowed destiny.

You wake up with an epiphany—you are one among
    many,
Your extraordinary talents somehow become
    mundane,
You start rubbing shoulders with a bunch of morons
Who have short-sightedness and mock at your
    strongs.

You feel as if this was all you had strived hard for,
Filtering all odds, you had to handle such
    parochial minds,
Backbiting, jealousy and materialistic talks,
Where am I moving with these minds of rock?

Show me my new paths, a different plan I sense
Than just being caught up in the present and past
    tense.
Something more intense, engaging and meaningful,
Far away from the meddling crowds, to a world more
    beautiful!

24

Indifferent Mysticism

Amidst the dilemma of big talks of achievement,
Lies the complex story of discontentment.
What a contrast in perceiving situations,
Two sets of people with different intuitions.

I wonder, if the most brilliant people in the system,
Live in a world of indifferent mysticism,
Where will the country and the world reach?
Is what I have to learn and you have to teach.

All say almost the same thing,
They seem like caged birds, circulating a ring.
Draw a tangent, get into action right away.
How long and far from the reality will you stay?

25

Journey of the Soul

An apt blend of human traits,
It moves from the lows to the greats.
It undergoes its natural process of evolution,
With multiple factors of predestined collusion.

Some fears that lurked years back,
Were all an in-built mechanism of its track,
To sculpt its spiritual, mental and physical forms,
To be able to see the roses amidst the thorns.

It freely mixes with the manifestations of the infinite,
Only to remain unchanged, to finally return to its incubation climate.
Is it a movement through eternity or a one-time affair?
There are many a questions in the miles to go before its clear.

26

The World Ahead

Challenges stand in front of the world ahead,
In an air of uncertainty, is the path being tread.
As mankind moves towards its state of natural
  predicament,
We now need a solution that is clearly instant.

Amidst vectors of personal and parochial interests,
With people entangled in a disease of mistrusts.
With all nations perceiving a threat from their angle,
They don't realize they are but stones studded in the
  same bangle.

How I wish the fissures heal very soon,
Global leadership needs to play its role in peak noon.
Efforts need to be multiplied along a single thread,
Human beings need to look beyond problems of
  mere butter and bread.

27

The Nilgiris: A Deeper Experience

The Majestic, the Beautiful, a site to behold,
Revealing a mystery untold.
This facet of nature is so pristine,
I am merely left bedazzled thinking!

Apart from the story of those dreadful leeches,
To just be here is a lesson that the Nilgiri teaches.
The tale of the still mountains, the moving clouds
    and breeze,
You are one of its all—the birds, the track and the
    trees!

The sight, the flavour is so tranquil,
As you tread, it is an inexpressible thrill.
Suddenly cut off from the cacophonic world,
You must let go to heal your soul!

28

Cacophony

As I withdraw from my surroundings around,
I don't know if it's right, lest I run aground.
Here I need you to anchor my steps ahead,
New paths, new vectors emerge in the path I tread.

It is in these times that I have found you closest to me,
Unto you I bow, all my steps reach to thee.
So, free me now from all my limitations,
I don't want to relive the painful past, no imitations.

You have put me among people with extreme negativity,
My job is to show up with a fresh positivity.
Sometimes, I wonder obtusely to myself,
After achieving my desires, will I abandon everything, set it to fire?

To surrender my soul to that fire, which will never tire,
In this conflict of materialism versus spiritualism, entangled in a mysticism of altruism
I feel so disinterested in this temporary world, so plastic, so full of pretence,
We all look like caricatures, each trying to outsmart the other with or for no end.

Amidst this cacophony of my life at this moment,
You beckon me to look ahead and not lament.
As I battle a few of my inherent weakness,
My only attempt is to disband that army of fears with keenness.

I wish to march towards my goal with absolute clarity,
It is incomprehensible at times, they are but obstacles on my way,
Every new march comes across as a new challenge,
You reflect on a new combination of conflicting factors—a melange!

29

The Wildlife

Silently you reside, away from the hustle-bustle,
A world entirely different, disjunctive from the city's whistle.
The frame speaks a million stories to my soul,
In this rhythm to which its entities do their rock and roll.

The same sun that shines through the city light,
Is the one that gives the flora and fauna its might.
The crisp rays of sun piercing through the lush green,
Was it reality or did I just wake up to a dream?

The elements in wildlife bear semblance to man's life,
The mighty prowls, the survival of the fittest,
Are all traits of the homo sapiens—the species with the IQ richest.
I wonder if we've really evolved, or are we in our times thickest?

30

The World Looks So Wide

When my fears block my communication route,
Deep down, I hear the sweet melody of a flute.
My mind questions You of your mysteries,
The evolved, the non-evolved and their intertwined astrologies!

The moment these expressions are no longer controllable,
I question you Lord—will I get any answer some day?
Are these thoughts just futile, of my mind so fertile?
Or I just wait and wait—keep putting some or the other paper weight!

I know not where I come from, when will I head?
I have just this moment here as a thread.
It wants to latch on to something, to be able to swim against the tide,
The path looks too unfamiliar, the world looks so wide.

31

Buddies

'Buddies'—a word so warm yet fun,
Anything, at anytime, you can share under the sun.
During gruesome pain, they will be your balm,
In sunny times, they cheer to vodka, wine and rum!

Seasons change, reasons change and so does the
    world,
Come what may, they will always make you bold!
You have fought and laughed, and may have terribly
    cried,
To bring a smile on your face, a friend has always
    tried!

I wonder why is a lover so different from a friend?
To cause hurt, is that his inherent trend?
He comes in life like a gust of wind,
Your happiness, your peace, why does he hinder?

It's a blessing to have the best of the two,
God has given this to only a few.
Is it possible to have a lover and a best friend
In the same person—who always has himself to lend?

32

Beckoning the Indian Women

You contributed immensely to the freedom struggle,
Broke the imperial chain of bondage with all might,
How finely you took the side of the right,
How marvellously you marched with men side by side!

You played your role so remarkably,
You pacified the most broken factions of those times.
How beautifully was the fabric of freedom embroidered!
Even though you had no education or training imparted.

What happened at the stroke of the midnight hour?
When India arose to life and freedom...
Where were you when you should have been there?
At the door of independence, you held back that very step.

Today your free spirit is dampened by unrelenting fear,
Your voice is merely like a bird in despair.
Why, even after conquering the sturdy heights of fame,
Is she still looked down upon as a Second Citizen?

Rapes, acid attacks, female feoticide and abuse,
How her body and spirit bleeds today so profuse!

33

The Five Elements of Life

Elements—the five basic constituents of the
   manifest,
Intertwining in a synchronized balance
To support the various life forms across the universe,
As the foundation of creations that have ever existed.

Earth—the grounding element and the base.
To hold onto the superstructure above it,
To bind the desired, the vital for life to exist,
To be able to let go of what one cannot resist.

Air—the life form in motion to circulate.
To always create space in every aspect of life,
To lighten and brighten the dampened spirit,
To infuse freshness of a new life after death.

Water—the cooling agent in the cycles of movement
That what markets the greatest constituent,
That's what quenches and causes turbulence,
A connection with the inner and the outer.

Fire—the glowing desire, hope and aspiration.
To the unmatchable speed that it can undertake,
The digestive force, the passion yet the warmth,
That what destroys to create, the element difficult to satiate.

Space—the mysterious yet integral component
Can take up any shape, be anything—a force to reckon,
The unheard sound, the matterless matter, the vacuum that creates the channel for the multiverse,
'Space'—an element impossible to trace.

34

Fallacies Fade

*L*ike a mirror that gathers dust over time,
The river that cuts through the mountains,
Carrying debris, soil—its experiences, gushing out,
Only to reach a point of clarity and crystallization.

Life goes on, so does the soul in its encounters
Accumulate the undesired and the unwanted.
However, juxtaposed is a place in eternity,
Apparently, an insignificant dot—in reality and expose.

The amalgamation of all colours—bright and dark,
The interplay of both joys and sorrows alike,
The meeting place of birth and death overlapped,
The blend of activity and nothingness entwined.

It is a marvel where indeed all 'fallacies fade',
A new life, new day, new freshness—what more!
The pulse of the universe resonates at a high
    frequency,
You circle back to the same with an unparalleled
    proficiency.

35

Oh Warrior!

Rise, oh Warrior! You are not done yet.
Your goals, the path of joy, you have still to tread.
So what, if there was a dark and scary storm,
Haven't you in the past fought all the norms?

Look behind, you have come a long way strong,
Where have you lost that confidence? Here you are wrong!
Refocus the present and future, readjust your sail,
Many enemies you are yet to nail.

Rest, relax, calm down if you must,
Look inside and thus, divine's path you must trust,
Believe in the vision you strive so hard for,
Recheck, there is so much of energy in store.

Safe, at Last

Sometimes, before you realize where you are,
Times have changed and you have come so far.
Turbulence amidst your journey strong,
From a state of comfort, you are about to drown!

You grasp for air, the push is stronger,
The stream gusts against your strength,
You fight, you resist with all your might,
Your breath is shallow and heartbeat high!

This state continues for quite a while,
Till the moment of realization, then you smile,
The way out of the whirlpool is non-resistance,
To go with the tide, embracing its essence!

Slowly, with the tide you swim through,
A piece of rope you finally hit through,
The magic wand plays its destined play,
Then, before you realize, on a safe island you happily
    lay!

Your Gratuity

The mystery has never completely unfolded,
To balance the energies, all through it is coded.
Perhaps, it must stay that way in its status quo,
So that its interplay, its equilibrium, is always on the go.

As a small baby, I take to my teething,
In this spiritual journey—for my destined meeting.
At times, you feel all in the know,
Only to infer that your understanding is still low!

There are many obstacles to overcome ahead,
You must, however, remain attached to that 'thread'.
In this execution of materialism and spirituality,
Your earnings through 'His' name will be your melody!

38
Your Grandeur!

I feel like writing incessantly for you, oh Lord!
Your praise, however, cannot be simply locked,
In a few words—I am trying to infer the same,
As you put me through my predestined game.

I know not where to stop and put my pen down,
For the abundance, the magnificence that wears the crown.
For the Master in whose presence you ever-smile,
Even if the situation around compels you to frown!

Hold me forever and protect me with your guidance,
I am your clueless child, without your presence.
Not an inch can anything move without your magic wand,
For you can bestow evergreen waters to the sand.

39
Transformation

A word that resonates strongly with every soul,
As it marches ahead against all tolls,
Only its destination it moves towards,
For there aren't any back—only forwards!

Just like a caterpillar feels all is done now,
The butterfly emerges with a beautiful bow.
We move through Nature's ordained path,
The splashing energy of change is a mandatory bath.

Some colours you adorn bright with might,
Yet, some are those dark ones that complement the light.
Both are significant in their own respective ways,
For you have to catch the mind in the direction it sways.

Are We Guilty?

Everyone now walks around hiding their faces,
The genesis of this new way, holistically needs traces.
What went wrong in the path we chose over centuries?
When we were all busy filling our treasures.

The stupidity of mankind has brought us here,
Why is it now that we should not fear?
Mother Nature had warned us in her subtleness,
We had all but neglected our own wellness.

Her rage, her bitterness, is perhaps justified,
Her ways, history has very well testified.
We are stuck in the ignorance of things,
Let's fold our hands and pray at home—we'll have to wait and watch lessons that times will bring!

41
Nature's Release

Ah! The Earth just relaxed and told us to do so too,
She said—go back and get into your right shoe.
Every once in a while, this play has to be staged,
To set things right, she has to be enraged.

The primitive life appears so beautiful and calm,
As if our painful life got its natural balm.
The air, the water, the food—all taste so pure,
We had gone astray—the wrong way forever.

Everything so important suddenly becomes futile,
Health first—rest all things can wait as we readjust
    our building tile.
The foundation needs to be recast yet again,
If we want to muddle through this self-inflicted pain.

42

The Fathomable Spirit

We live as if we were to live forever,
We challenge our demons, we fight and proceed,
Success is quantified in terms of riches and positions,
The unfathomable spirit is looked up to with no
   inhibitions!

We live in our pride with a false sense of ego,
We are never satisfied, more and more we want to
   grow.
Where we are heading, however, we do not know,
This pandemic was as if an unthought-of shot!

We need to humble and mellow down a bit,
If we want to successfully come out of this pit!
Who is the greater spirit, we are but a part,
We should be ready now, for the game is about to
   restart!

43

Change, No Alternative

*L*eaders, heads of states, all try to attempt their best,
To pull out the world from their destined test.
All efforts appear so absolute and futile,
It is time for the energy to appear versatile!

The challenges have changed their methodology,
We definitely need to devise a new pedagogy.
New ways of life now have to surface,
To compensate the damages that have been brought about.

Doctors and caregivers are pouring out their energies no doubt,
But this pandemic will require a greater shout out,
Healers and spiritual masters will now lose their backstage,
To decrystallize myths, busting a new adage!

44

It Is for Us Only

The wind of change now flows gently as a breeze,
The inanimate is animated—flowers and the trees.
The animate is inanimate—us the human beings.
The world will perhaps transform, remember, a lot
    many things.

The door that remained shut owing to pollution,
Now welcomes fresh air to the house.
Creativity in our minds had fizzled out,
The energy runs positive amidst this perspective
    bout.

Children who had not seen their parents since long,
The bonds of love in families had gotten strong.
The detoxification that Nature is undergoing,
Is reflective in the ways of life so rejuvenating.

Primitive: An Era Evergreen

I am reminded deeply of our ancestral lineage,
When we were primitive—no futile baggage.
Eat, drink and sleep with awareness—no worries,
What has man himself created—artificial monies!

He ruins his life chasing his own creations,
Trying to find happiness and contentment in this chase.
Whole births through, he is himself lost in this self-created maze.
Alas, the most superior species has lost its way!

Mother Nature, like a mother always pulls back her child,
She keeps a discreet eye, even while they are in the wild.
We, as her children, must now exhibit prudence and live
Up to her expectations with our divine intelligence!

46

A New Way of Life

*F*or the first time, everything is changing en bloc,
The impact on lifestyles, businesses, politics, et al.
Hope mankind is able to stand tall,
To the test of times that we have been put to.

It is eerie to think about this change so massive,
We have dealt our cards which were not so
    impressive.
Now, we adapt to the new ways of living,
Which are perhaps far beyond mere cravings!

He alone knows how many will survive and perish,
The times ahead, challenge-wise are very lavish,
With folded hands and a guilty spirit, oh Lord!
Mankind prays and pleads its case, my Lord!

47

Eyes that Couldn't See

Elderly, gloomy eyes look through their spectacles,
Masks cover their noses and lungs of low capacity.
They carry their daily grocery bags close to their
    body,
Despite no fear or threat of any robbery.

The crime has been committed together as a race,
Now, the aftermaths every individual has to face.
It doesn't matter how much or little you were wrong,
This current of uncertainty will only make us strong.

Times can be so unpleasant and ruthless,
No one had ever in their wildest of imagination
    cared less,
Or foreseen this paradox of life so marvellous,
I only wonder, how we could all have been fearless!

48

The Predestined Meeting

*Y*ouths must meet their predestined old age,
That's the order of nature that we have adhered to.
Old clothes must be discarded for the new,
A mystery which has cleared only for a few.

We live like we'll never die and die like we've never
    lived,
Why is this irony, my Lord? Tell me please.
Youth passes by running and old age by thinking,
The entire persona of life is just in an eye's winking.

To have not felt your presence, oh Lord!
Is to have lived only watching the cloud.
Without the silver lining, life is fleeting,
One must prepare with love for 'the predestined
    meeting'.

49

Longingness Revisited

Let me dive into your ocean of infinite love,
My love for you merges into the yearning vastness.
I cannot describe in words my emotions so intense,
It is only through an inward journey one can sense.

My creator, caregiver and owner of what I have,
You have always made me feel your presence in my life.
Continue to do so more and more ahead,
How can I forget your protective hand which has led?

Words are just sublime, it is difficult to capture.
The longing waves hit against the shore to merge,
Only to recede into the maze of life,
Tasting a sip of the nectar so divine and pristine!

50
Is the Path Ahead Backwards?

This battle of the haves and have-nots,
Is entangled in complex knots.
No one knows when this inequality will stop,
Drenched in the sweat and blood are many a clot!

Whichever way the world goes or the universe,
This gap of non-possession they will never traverse.
Any change, with positive or negative impact,
Their struggles and hardships, I will forever respect!

Millions of us are blessed, yet billions of us perhaps not,
Why this skewed distribution of your blessings, oh Lord?
Why are things created this very way?
The price for which one set always has to pay!

Why not have an egalitarian system that was primitive?
No colour, no gender, no caste—all equity.

Please foster this energy towards the new world,
As I humbly request, oh Lord, to take everything
into your fold!

Another Dimension

At times, a new dimension of life opens up,
Where there is nothing, yet everything.
Amidst the confusion and chaos—a serenity.

Our conscience very rarely reaches this point,
Most of us, most of the time, are stuck in the joint.
It is difficult to concentrate on the element,
As many other irrelevant things disguise as relevant.

This stage comes rarely to put it straight,
All of us keep transiting different gates.
Sages, saints and holy men are indeed very blessed,
They, after a few cycles of births and deaths, are totally refreshed.

Life: A Meandering River

Life—over the years—an untold mystery,
At times it's so simple like a piece of your pastry.
At times it puts you into a maze,
Running behind things you should not chase.

There are people who pretend till the last minute,
Yet blessed souls never make you cry, even in a
    gimmick.
Life is complex, with its own given choices,
To choose the right one is your luck among million
    voices.

You hold the beliefs, your visions held high,
Life gives you jolts, you can only sigh.
You must pull up your strengths then,
Because there are fewer who can offer a helping hand.

Hold on to that subtle piece of thread,
Long miles to go, a long path to tread.
Stay close, stay firm to the voice within,
For, gradually and craftily, your life is knitting.

53

The Sun at Dawn

The magnificence par excellence you behold,
The only time you let yourself be rolled.
You emerge calm in the spectacular scene,
As if scripting your self-created theme.

The grandeur of your presence rises in a minute,
The entire day you shine bright till sunset.
The reddish hue mesmerizes me deep,
It challenges my imagination, extremely steep.

The power sustaining all life forms on Earth,
Everything will definitely go extinct with your dearth.
A condensed source of energy so intense,
A story full of mystery that cannot be put forth in any sentence.

No matter how many words I write about your might,
One can only infer once they have your sight.

You do not let yourself be known to all,
As your magnanimous spirit runs through the
universe tall.

Significance of Rain

As I sip my hot cup of coffee this early morning,
The rain beautifully falls on the lovely tree.
Some drops fall in a train while others cling on only in vain
The wind plays its music and the rain its lyrics.

Some memories arise from the days gone by,
As the cup transitions from warm to cold now.
Of meetings that shouldn't have happened but did,
As the rain makes my walk on the memory lane skid.

However, it washes down the dirt stuck in the past,
Which got accumulated in a life that ran too fast.
Perhaps, as if in a play, with an ever-changing cast,
My imagination now runs deep with a vision vast.

Mankind: Yet to Arrive

Zillions of mysteries lie folded ahead,
Mankind yet has several universes to tread.
We are but a speck in the entire frame,
Our imagination is a storehouse we need to tame.

Some think that we have come a long, long way,
Scientific inventions and discoveries have made our
    minds sway.
For what we know is only the tip of the iceberg,
All that we have reached is the sentinel framework.

His grace will show us the trajectory we follow,
Our own self-inflated egos we must mellow.
Nature, on its own, is the rule maker and game
    changer,
We are merely the followers and at best harbingers.

Let Me be Your Light

*Y*ou choose your harbingers selectively, I know,
One needs to be non-qualified in the modern ways.
No amount of degree and education can let the
    illusion sway,
For the ways are yours and syllabus untold.

Purity of heart is the sole interview I infer,
The regular way is not yours—it does totally differ.
One is caught unaware when the spotlight falls,
When your name the grace of the divine has called.

Blessed are those few who have all unlearnt,
After experiencing the pain has got hands burnt.
The melody of life then plays for them,
In ways and happenings, they would have never
    dreamt.

Art Forms

*L*onging for the art so pristine and pious,
Transmitted across generations as a treasure.
To experience it requires tremendous grace,
When God gives you, just simply embrace.

The role of a guru cannot be understated,
These are living forms that are never intimated.
To reach the zenith should be one's aim,
For once you touch it, you will never be the same.

Some have given their life to this,
Not experiencing it shows that some thing's amiss,
They attempted, they practiced and they gave it all,
The scenario that they are in, they can never fall.

Institutions

'Institutions'—they have withstood the test of time,
Yet contribute so much to the misery of mind.
Flawed concepts that ruin lives have sustained,
Was this struggle always ordained?

Many a thinkers have supported institutionalism,
Not realizing the rigidity and resistance it brings.
Every system, culture, ethos and fabric should evolve,
Else, it is meaningless and must dissolve!

Several women, caged like animals in it,
To give false sanctity, the societal norms it feeds.
Spiritual structures are another set of misogynists,
Carpeting many a lies and patriarchists.

Every woman fights it her entire life,
In each role, that of a daughter, mother or wife.
This feminine power if one can ever accumulate,
The dance the world will witness is one that will
    emancipate.

59

Life: Certainty versus Uncertainty

What is this mystery called Life?
Had read somewhere, it is the uncertainty,
Between two certain points of birth and death.
How fleetingly futile it appears yet unexplored!

Why is it that we have always lived less?
There is always something unabsorbed,
Something not enjoyed—but always missed.
Why is it that we are not when the moment kissed?

We, at times, crib about life's struggles and troubles,
Not knowing that it is merely a short-lived bubble.
Before we know, this stay is not eternal,
Let us live wholeheartedly before the effervescence
    fizzles.

Social or Unsocial Media?

Social media has made us go bonkers,
Trying to create a virtual reality without vectors.
But for the doze of information it imparts,
A fake identity blooms, the real one it discards.

Life is lost between a few likes and dislikes,
Anyone and everyone can now hold a mike.
Real understanding and analysis is at bay,
A Frankenstein's monster is created—what more can
   I say!

Youth is lost in uploading fabricated moments,
In reality, the days pass by in torments.
No one realizes what a web we have created,
Only to end up with harm which is self-inflicted.

Surprisingly, people love this pseudo world,

What is the significance of the word 'social'?
When all you do is end up in a bottle.
The cage looks good initially, with no outlets
    definitely.

What is so social about its name?
Social or truly unsocial could become its meme.
It disconnects real social behaviours,
Only to connect unreal, unsocial misbehaviours!

༄

61

Keep Your Spirit High

While riding on a high, all seems fine,
Life is blooming and brimming all the time.
When the tide recedes, however,
Everything seems done with forever.

How pitiable the situation becomes suddenly,
As if nothing is left in life, it's a comedy!
In the gravest and gloomiest moments of life,
You have no option but to surrender to faith.

Many a times, such a phase has come to me,
Don't know this time, when I will be free.
A real test of patience one has to give,
If there is desire and fire to live!

Your inner battle you alone put up a fight with,
The warrior of light eventually moves out of the pit.
Outer or inner—both are tough though,
For only after this victory, the path will show.

Never put your sword down, oh fighter!
The weather will change and get better.
You will find kindred souls on the way,
Together you will proceed following the ray.

The company of good souls—noble and kind,
Will always keep your sanity in mind.
Even if you are put through a grind,
To the eternal source of power they will bind!

62

Quarantine Reflections I

My little 10×10 room—how much do I talk to you?
I know every inch of you by now,
Of every detail of paint and objects in you
All objects tell their story—me included now!

The scariest one being the pulse oximeter,
A wonderful toy for the corona-inflicted population.
It beeps and beats, till your heart skips a beat,
Oh believe me, scoring above 90s was not limited to academics!

A corona patient sits for this exam every two hours,
And the funniest part is the exam, examinee and examiner are one.
These is no delay in the preparation, question paper and the result,
But the minute you put your finger, the parameters misbehave.

Einstein left at the right time,
Else he would have scratched his head on the memes.
The so-called wonder little machines in my room,
I hope you do not multiply to a hospital and mushroom.

Then I get bored of this oximeter and move on to a thermometer,
This serious object shoots and at times just doesn't.
The ping-pong of the multigrade fever and weakness,
These little objects mock at human nature's tenderness.

Then comes my favourite—the blood pressure apparatus,
My old friend since two years.
Its mocking behaviour I am well conversant with
In my 10×10 space, the only friend I get along with.

The sanitizer bottle mocks me—write something about me!
The knight in shining armour fighting these invisible microbes
Has given dollars to its manufacturers,

It laughs and says, 'lotions and creams have never
   been your benefactors!'

Next comes the multicoloured pills,
Zincovit, the little red riding hood with the orange
   Vitamin C,
The gross Ivermectin numbing my nerves,
I wish it was never discovered to serve.
Doxy is a gentle girl wearing a red and black dress,
Evion—the Vitamin E green guy to ensure none
   happens to come out in distress.

Now comes Mr Mask, who recently had lost its
   importance,
And now ensured all above got their true significance
Kuch khataa humnein aur kuch tumne bhi ki hogi,
Aise hi nahin corona ki sazaa mili hogi.

The harmless steamer—a solace for me,
By using it, I feel so mentally free.
The most effective object among all,
It stands out, intangibly tall.

I wonder when this quarantine will end,
I pray this passes peacefully, without any tear rolling
   down.

It has been long since I held my daughter close to
    my heart,
I hear her cries of separation since the quarantine's
    start.

It is not easy to stay isolated and hear ambulances
    passing by,
Prayers, prayers and prayers—the world needs as the
    population cries.
Almighty! I hope we will not be more sinned than
    sinning,
Reignite that divine light which in us is dimming.

The pace at which loved ones are leaving,
And the variegated ways in which the virus is
    multiplying,
Things seem out of control in these moments,
But you have held your children close in torrents!

I pray this second wave recedes fast,
With your magical touch and grace, this tough time
    won't last.
Doctors are angels you have sent from above,
Mellow down please, in these times we need more
    love.

'Sorry' would mean a small word for the mistakes we have done,
After stealing the treasures from Mother Nature, where would we run?
Overexploitation, resource imbalance, skewed developments and greed,
The list is endless I realize—we now truly shun!

Quarantine Reflections II

Sleepy, lousy days and nights pass by,
All things in life come unexpected as one tries.
Solitude kisses when one is entangled in busyness,
Busyness kisses when one truly seeks solitude!

Wish this time passes off well and reflective,
Auspicious days of Navratri begin perfective.
May Goddess Durga bestow her divine grace,
No more coronavirus in the world we would trace!

The battle of good health has always been a mental one,
The desire for life in the fear of unknown,
The human spirit of never say die and strive,
History stands a witness, if in centuries we dive!

Life force exerts itself against a challenging era,
Every fighter proudly wears his or her tiara.
We have come a long, long way,
Several set of monsters we humans have beheaded!

Love in the Times of Covid-19

Caught unaware in the dexterity of time,
Human population had thought, 'all is mine'.
Love had transformed into greed and lust,
Mother Nature has indeed lost her trust!

There is an inherent need to revisit that abode,
As we stand here juxtaposed on crossroads.
Laws of love are clearly being rewritten,
While under the burden of our wrongs, we lay
    smitten!

Virtual love will no longer hold grounds,
Either with other humans or with Nature abound.
Compassion sun-kissed with empathy is all we need,
Let us all pledge to sow a sustainable seed!

The fear of death has brought us close to love for
    life,
Nature has made us understand in nervous ways rife.
Love is what an angel doctor manifests,

By keeping every patient close to her breast!

Fear not, oh human consciousness, let your mettle show,
In this facade of Covid-19 illness, to weakness we shall not bow.
Embrace that divine light—oh warrior,
Break the chains of anything unlike love or any barrier!

65

Discriminate Covid-19, Not Its Warriors

'Discrimination'—a word that cuts and undercuts,
An all-pervasive phenomenon shaking your guts.
Insecurity and fear of the human mind,
Futile, painful memories it can wind!

Never had I felt ever so great,
Till I contracted Covid-19 for my ill fate.
A social stigma even among the educated,
Their education is now clearly wasted!

Your perception colours your rational wisdom,
You are subjected to unwanted criticism.
It's a mere novel disease in the human evolution,
Which makes it so blown out of proportion.

Come on, use the precautions, you definitely must,
Do not let your eyes subject other people to dust.
For heaven's sake, discriminate against the illness,
And only pray for other people's wellness!

A Deeper Meaning

Childhood passes by waiting to mature,
Those naive years simply flash by.
Under the protection of parents' wings,
Before you realize, adulthood springs.

You toil for your inner battles,
Outer ones always show their mettle.
Between these transitions, you catch a shore,
Professional and financial security you store.

The next ladder of marriage comes,
Some drown in it while others jump.
Middle age then strikes hard,
You end up calculating your losses and gains.

Unfortunately, ills, bills and pills only remain,
While you were just catching a train.
You then realize, to give a deeper meaning to life,
You are then taken care of, if lucky, by your wife.

Life needs to be eventually rewritten,
With a grander purpose and a broader vision.
We needn't just simply exist as life happens,
Rather live and enjoy as it happens.

Create beautiful memories and live fullest,
Resonate with its rhythm as you enjoy its fragrance.
Enrich its experience by touching hearts,
Go back to the ecstasy from where it all starts.

Blissful Praise

My eyes await your arrival one fine day,
Every moment, the heart yearns for your thoughts.
Masters and spiritual guides say it is easy,
For mortals like us, you seem way too busy.

My spiritual journey though short it may be,
It is pure and blissful, echoing the depth.
Divinity—I have experienced in my own subtle
　　ways,
Just as how a pendulum sways.

I know not if I will ever reach that epitome,
May be in this lifetime or several more to come.
Intuition in me catches certain flavours,
I feel like a child playing with colours.

You feel as if you are painting the canvas,
Not knowing that the divine hand holds your little
　　hand,
It is His interplays that you view as your own,

For He is the magician who owns the show you
    perform.

All His expectation from you is to remember Him,
Utter praises and words of sweetness in His name.
Thank Him for what all He has magnanimously
    manifested,
For He is the Creator as well as the Created!

68

A Yearning Soul

My naive steps try to somehow find You,
I search here and there as I miss You.
Like a parted lover's yearnings for warmth,
Of love and affection sealing separation's wrath!

I call out to You by different names,
Try to remember You in every breath I take.
To attempt unfolding this mystical facade,
With devotion and love brought on record!

Various art forms—dance, music and all,
I try to master each one without fall.
My mind interprets them as ways to You,
I must confess that it is absolutely true!

The love for the known yet partially unknown,
The quest for balance in dichotomy,
The paint of conjunction of all opposites,
The merger of the source and the sink alike.

The epitome of mysticism of longing merger,
The desire to get hold of the greatest treasure.
How a child yearns for their mother's love,
My soul in front of the Infinite bows.

69

The River: The Ocean

I stop, reflect and absorb where I am,
Life has moved fast and slow—both!
Like the course of a river originating from source,
Waterfalls, rapids, stagnation—yet moving multiple shores.

I accumulate, I release, I splash, I cut through,
I am a river—both mighty and weak,
But ever connected to my origin.
The beginning and end are both so intense and immense.

I give birth to tributaries who will find their way,
This beautiful dimension of life opens a new channel.
Of reserved energies harnessed to a larger potential,
The river always reignites its origin, for its existence is essential!

In my course when I run silent, I run deep,
When I am restless, I run fast—balancing the acts.
The river—a metaphor for my life wearing varied
   hats,
The River is me, and the Ocean, thee!

∽

70

Playfulness

I want to touch the very depths of life,
But I hold back the urge before I purge.
Exploration does not come easy at all,
It is an art to balance successive falls.

Solitude, extreme ones, exposes you to ventures,
Truly, they aren't cakewalk adventures.
A very delicate rope one treads on,
Sometimes, not realizing time's turn from dusk to
    dawn.

A fleeting moment of depth and stillness,
Eradicates decades and decades of dullness.
You come back to life soaked in grace,
This illusion of life and death—you again embrace!

71

Why?

I try to seek you in the rigmarole of life,
Seconds here and there—I steal for you.
What an irony of being it is, my creator!
You leave us to be only longing for You!

Why do you create us when the goal is You?
Why do we experience falsehood when the truth is
    You?
Why do we suffer when it is only temporary?
Why the illusion when there is no test?

Why is there war when the search is for peace?
Why is there night when it is only the absence of
    light?
Why is there marriage when you come and go alone?
Why is there life when certainty is death?

Why are there diseases when equilibrium is easy?
Why are there misunderstandings when
    understanding is the way?

Why is there inequality when all are born equal?
Why is there sadness when it is happiness we seek?

The questions question me deep,
When will I get my answers and sleep?
The waves I ride everyday—up and down,
As I pray daily to the Almighty who wears the crown.

72

March of the Feminine

*T*he struggle of this generation's women,
Who have been raised to be strong,
To fight undauntingly against the wrong,
To witness a society in transition, perhaps too long.

We will no doubt create stronger women,
Yet equally strong men.
To stand firmly, not essentially quintessential Indian
    men,
A vibrant feminine ethos in Indian culture is our
    gem.

Revisiting our heritage is the need today,
To proudly be able to showcase to the world.
To unleash the inner strength we behold,
To unfold a history never been told.

73

Twin Saga

My mind oscillates between harmony and chaos,
The balance of sanity and insanity of the world.
We are but mere microbes in this gigantic ecosystem,
Sometimes all, sometimes nothing to fathom.

This complex mystery of lives and deaths,
You feel you have captured the depths.
The next moment, one is back to square one,
To do the done undone and the undone done.

We move through this complex web of mysticism,
It is as if looking through a massive prison.
Multiple universes, multiple lives exist,
The hand of the Almighty in all realms persist.

The solution to this complexity, however, is basic,
Neither Vedic nor too algebraic,
Surrender with absolute devotion to the power,
The grace of the universe will forever shower.

74

Ignorance is Bliss

Had heard once that 'ignorance is bliss',
The more we seek to know the future,
The lesser we seek to want it.
Mystery is the way and should always remain.

Predictors and fortune tellers tell,
What is written in one's destiny will eventually yell.
No matter what course we try to correct,
God's plan is always accurate and perfect.

The plan spans over lifetimes together,
We only know the path of this lifetime.
The theory of karma and *sanskara*s,
We only understand the *alankara*s.

So, what is the way forward then?
His or Her name and grace is the mend.
Are we the puppets or the puppeteers?
May these doubts forever disappear.

Life from Pram to Wheelchair

The uncertainty between two certain points,
The attempt to predict it and control,
A blend of predetermination and will power,
Guided by the Divine as a watch tower.

Physically and emotionally, it starts and finishes identically,
The journey from a pram to a wheel chair.
The return to the point of innocence again,
The cacophony passes by in a jiffy even if you refrain.

The baldness, the immobility, the toothlessness, the indigestion,
The need for care and love—the world's entry and exit merge.
The heaviness of life collapses to a bubble,
To yet another transactional shift of a baby's gurgle!

Acknowledgements

I sincerely thank my family, my siblings Chand Chopra and Anish Chopra, my loving daughter Hazel and all my loved ones who have stood by me through thick and thin. This book would not have been possible without you. I acknowledge the constant support and guidance of all my teachers, who have refined my knowledge, language and personality over the years. I am grateful for those bittersweet moments in my life which led me to introspect and write these contemplative poems. I am thankful to the hard work put in by the incredible team at Rupa Publications, who shaped this beautiful book which is now in your hands. I truly hope you will enjoy reading my life's literary masterpiece called *The Mosaic*.

Thank you.